Perfect Plays for Building Vocabulary

10 Short Read-Aloud Plays With Activity Pages That Teach 100+ Key Vocabulary Words in Context

Justin McCory Martin

■ SCHOLASTIC

NEW YORK • TORONTO • LONDON • AUCKLAND • SYDNEY
MEXICO CITY • NEW DELHI • HONG KONG • BUENOS AIRES

Cover and interior design by Maria Lilja
Illustrations by Constanza Basaluzzo

ISBN: 978-0-545-15048-4

Contents

Introduction

Perfect Plays for Building Vocabulary, Grades 3-4 is a collection of funny, memorable short plays designed to support your classroom vocabulary instruction by giving your students the opportunity to interact with a wide variety of essential vocabulary words in an active and authentic way.

Each play teaches eight to ten vocabulary words that third and fourth graders need to know as they move forward into more complex reading material. Filled with talking robots, dodge-ball-playing dragons, and monsters who love to cook, these short plays are designed to hold students' interest through multiple readings. Your students will enjoy reading the plays aloud together as a class, taking on characters and trying out new voices. The classroom activities that follow each play—such as fun crossword puzzles, word searches, and match-ups—give students a chance to practice using, writing, spelling, and defining the new words they are learning.

At the same time, *Perfect Plays for Building Vocabulary* and the corresponding activities also help students build listening comprehension and fluency skills.

Here are five keys to vocabulary learning to remember:

Revel in Words

Teach your students to pay attention to new words. There can be a tendency for young readers to skip over unfamiliar words as they listen or read. Encourage your students to listen for and celebrate new words. When a student uses or finds a great new word, write it on the board, add it to your Word Wall, or challenge students to use it in a sentence! Soon, your students will be "tuned in" to vocabulary.

Mix Up Your Methods

Direct instruction of key vocabulary is often essential to a lesson. You can't learn geography without studying terms like *longitude* and *latitude*. However, formal study is usually insufficient for students to add new words to their permanent vocabulary. Students need to hear, read, write, and say a word many times in order to own it.

Go Beyond Definitions

To truly know a word, students need to be able to do more than offer up a remembered definition; they need to be able to use it! That is, they need to understand the word's logical relationship to other words and understand how the word functions in different contexts.

Repeat, Repeat, Repeat

The best way to learn a word is to run into it often. Give your students opportunities to encounter words repeatedly and in a variety of contexts.

Read at School and at Home

The great majority of a child's vocabulary growth occurs incidentally. Words are gained by listening and in conversation, but mostly through reading. Independent reading at home and at school is essential for building the strong vocabulary that will help students succeed on standardized tests and in middle school, high school, and beyond.

10 Tips for Teaching With the Vocabulary Plays in This Book

The vocabulary plays in this book can be used in a variety of ways to enrich your student's word learning. Here are just a few:

① Model How to Read the Plays

Share the list of vocabulary words in the play that may be new to your students. Read each word aloud and talk about the strategies students can use to decode words they do not know—such as finding beginning or ending sounds, and breaking the word into parts. Read the first play aloud several times while students follow along. Use your readings to model how expression, pace, and inflection help communicate meaning. For example, take a sentence from the first play and read it slowly and then quickly. Read it quietly and then loudly and grumpily. Ask kids: *How does the way we read a line affect its meaning?* Then, invite kids to read aloud with you.

② Try Choral and Echo Reading

Choral and echo reading are great techniques for giving your students the repeated practice they need to really absorb new words. They also help to build fluency. To do choral reading, you and your students read together as a group. That way, all your students read at the same pace and with the same phrasing and intonation as the rest of the group. In echo reading, you read a line and students then repeat it, echoing your expression, tone, and pacing.

③ Assigning Roles

After you read the play aloud together, have students take turns reading the play aloud. If some of your students are reluctant to read aloud, assign two readers to each role. If you are using a document camera or projector, assign one student the role of "pointer." He or she can point to each line of dialogue in turn. If students have copies of the play, have them use highlighters to mark their passages. Give them time to read over their lines before reading it aloud.

④ Create a Role for the Dictionary

During some readings of the plays, you may want to assign a student or students the role of the Dictionary. The Dictionary halts the play reading and shares the definition of the vocabulary word. You might even want to challenge the Dictionary to answer any questions about the pronunciation or meaning of the vocabulary word.

Meeting the Common Core State Standards

Vocabulary is one of the foundational elements of the Common Core State Standards 2011 (corestandards.org) because it is essential to speaking, listening, and writing. Third and fourth graders must be able to:

- Determine or clarify the meaning of unknown and multiple-meaning words and phrases based on grade 4 reading and content, choosing flexibly from a range of strategies.

- Demonstrate understanding of figurative language, word relationships, and nuances in word meanings.

- Demonstrate understanding of words by relating them to their opposites (antonyms) and to words with similar but not identical meanings (synonyms).

- Acquire and use accurately grade-appropriate general academic and domain-specific words and phrases, including those that signal precise actions, emotions, or states of being (e.g., *quizzed*, *whined*, *stammered*) and that are basic to a particular topic (e.g., *wildlife*, *conservation*, and *endangered* when discussing animal preservation).

- Consult reference materials (e.g., dictionaries, glossaries, thesauruses), both print and digital, to find the pronunciation and determine or clarify the precise meaning of key words and phrases.

The plays and activities in this book were designed to meet the Common Core State Standards. Each play presents a carefully-chosen set of related vocabulary words and presents them in the context of an easy-to-read play. By studying related words together (e.g., *courteous* and *considerate*; *colossal* and *immense*), students are given the opportunity to distinguish precise shades of meaning. Multiple readings of the plays and completion of the activities give students the needed repetition that allows them to take an unfamiliar vocabulary word and make it their own.

Readers Theater

After you've done a few plays as a whole class, consider breaking your class into groups and having them perform the plays as Readers Theater. Group members can work together and decide how they want to perform the play. Encourage them to experiment and explore the characters. What voices will they use? How will they present the vocabulary words? The different performances of the same play will give students extra opportunities to hear and learn the vocabulary words.

Share the Wealth

Consider having your students perform their vocabulary plays for another class in the same grade or the grade below. Have your students who are playing the role of the Dictionary on hand to answer questions!

Grow Your Vocabulary Lists

Write the vocabulary list for each play on a piece of chart paper. That way, when your students discover another feeling word or weather word, you can add it to your growing list! By the end of the year, your lists of words could easily become twice as long.

Add Another Scene

In the Activities section after each play, you'll find three more related words. Challenge students to come up with an extra scene or extra lines of dialogue to incorporate these additional vocabulary words!

Write Your Own Vocabulary Plays (or Stories)

In the back of this book, you'll find six additional vocabulary word lists. Share one of the themed word lists with your students. Challenge them to write their own quick plays or short stories using as many new vocabulary words as they can.

Extra Vocabulary Challenge

Using the vocabulary word lists in the back of this book, invite students to design their own word searches, match-ups, or other puzzles for their peers. Students will gain great word practice as they design their own word-learning activities and do those created by their classmates.

© 2013 Scholastic Inc • *Perfect Plays for Building Vocabulary, Grades 3–4*

Vocabulary Word List for All Plays

Friendship words	kind • cooperative • share • courteous • dispute • lonely • considerate • loyal • generous • respect • trust
Neighborhood words	neighbor • pedestrian • volunteer • stroll • traffic • community • mayor • statue • avenue • civic • vehicle
Family words	reunion • grandfather • aunt • cousin • relative • toddler • festive • tradition • ancestor • infant • sibling
Big words, small words	humongous • length • gigantic • massive • minuscule • miniature • colossal • height • gargantuan • immense • microscopic
Feeling words	miserable • confidence • jealous • proud • grumpy • cozy • embarrassed • emotion • baffled • delighted • glum
Words for heroes and villains	villain • courageous • rescue • evil • vile • honor • coward • bravery • loathsome • scoundrel • virtuous
Movement words	skid • spring • sluggish • rapid • soar • dart • halt • swift • bound • cling • lunge
Weather words	sweltering • gust • tornado • temperature • drizzle • forecast • humid • blizzard • drought • frigid • icicle
Animal words	nocturnal • pounce • enormous • predator • species • venomous • keen • scurry • burrow • camouflage • migrate
Cooking words	apron • ingredient • grind • boil • dash • recipe • edible • bon appetit • culinary • scrumptious • season

Cave Kids

CHARACTERS

Narrator	Bop	Ted
Jenna	Sot	Trish
Teacher	Gorp	

Teacher: We have three new students in our class. They are cave kids. They are here from the Stone Age. Let's be **kind** to these new kids. Let's make them feel at home.

kind (*adj.*, kinde): helpful; friendly; good

Narrator: It was time for the class to work in groups of four. One group was made up of Jenna and the three cave kids.

Jenna: We need to write a story as a group.

Bop: I don't want to.

© 2013 Scholastic Inc. • Perfect Plays for Building Vocabulary, Grades 3–4

Jenna:	But it's time to write a story.
Sot:	I think I will draw a picture.
Jenna:	We need to work as a group. I hope all of you will help me.
Gorp:	I want to take a nap.
Jenna:	You are new at this school. I want to be friends with you. But you are not being very **cooperative**.

cooperative (*adj.*, koh-op-ur-uh-tiv): helpful; willing to work together

Narrator:	Then, it was time for the class to play outside. The kids were playing soccer. One of the cave kids grabbed the ball.
Bop:	This round thing is ours now.
Narrator:	Bop kicked the ball to Sot.
Sot:	Only the cave kids can play.
Narrator:	Sot kicked the ball to Gorp. Gorp sat on the ball.
Gorp:	This makes a nice seat.
Ted:	You are new at this school. We want to be your friends. But it is nice to **share**. You need to share.

share (*verb*, shair): to receive, use, or enjoy together with another or others

Narrator:	The cave kids were not any better at lunch. They kept grabbing food from other kids' plates.
Bop:	I want to eat those little yellow things.
Narrator:	Bop grabbed a kid's corn on the cob and gobbled it up.

Sot:	I want to eat that round red thing.
Narrator:	Sot grabbed a kid's apple and gobbled it up.
Gorp:	I want that white food. It looks tasty.
Narrator:	Gorp grabbed a kid's napkin. Gorp gobbled it up!
Trish:	You are new at this school. We have tried to be your friends. But friends are **courteous** to each other. You are not courteous at all.

> **courteous** (*adj.*, kur-tee-uhs): polite and respectful

Jenna:	Friends are cooperative. You are not cooperative at all.
Ted:	Friends share. You do not share at all.
Narrator:	The cave kids had caused a big **dispute**. All the other kids were angry. They walked away. Now the cave kids were sitting by themselves.

> **dispute** (*noun*, diss-pyoot): an argument or fight

Bop:	This is not good.
Sot:	We have made everyone mad.
Gorp:	They have all walked away.
Bop:	I wanted to make new friends.
Sot:	I'm **lonely**.

> **lonely** (*adj.*, lone-lee): sad because you are all by yourself

Bop:	I have an idea. Let's make up a song.
Narrator:	You may not know this. Cave people are very good singers. After lunch, the cave kids sang their new song.

© 2013 Scholastic Inc • Perfect Plays for Building Vocabulary, Grades 3–4

The cave kids (*singing*):

> We are so sorry that we made you mad.
>
> We are so sorry that we made you sad.
>
> We come from caves. We come from the past.
>
> We want to make friends. We want them to last.

Teacher: That was very **considerate**. Thank you, cave kids.

considerate (*adj.*, kuhn-sid-uh-rit): careful to think about the feelings of others

Narrator: After that, the cave kids made lots of good friends. The cave kids made lots of **loyal** friends. Everyone liked the cave kids. But they *loved* their silly songs.

loyal (*adj.*, loi-uhl): showing faithfulness to someone or something

Word Challenge

Here are three more words having to do with friendship.
Can you use each word in a sentence?

generous (*adj.*, jen-ur-uhss): showing a willingness to give or share

respect (*verb*, ri-spekt): to show proper appreciation for someone or their feelings

trust (*verb*, truhst): to rely on or have confidence in someone

Bonus!

What words could you use to describe a good friend?

_____, _____, _____,

_____, _____

© 2013 Scholastic Inc • *Perfect Plays for Building Vocabulary, Grades 3–4*

Name _____

| Word Box | kind | cooperative | share | courteous | dispute | lonely | considerate | loyal |

Word Jumble

The letters of these vocabulary words are all mixed up. Using the word box above, figure out the correct answer and write it on the blank provided.

1. l y n e l o _____ meaning: *sad because you are all by yourself*

2. o c o u s u t r e _____ meaning: *polite and respectful*

3. l l y a o _____ meaning: *faithful*

4. d s u i t e p _____ meaning: *an argument or fight*

5. c p t i e r a o v e o _____ meaning: *helpful; willing to work together*

6. k d i n _____ meaning: *courteous and thoughtful to others*

7. h a e r s _____ meaning: *to enjoy with others*

8. c s i r a t e d e o n _____ meaning: *careful to think about the feelings of others*

Word Search

Using the word box above, can you find and circle the vocabulary words found from this unit?

E	V	I	T	A	R	E	P	O	O	C
B	L	I	V	U	S	G	D	V	D	N
L	O	Y	A	L	U	H	T	P	N	D
A	T	M	U	U	M	D	A	G	I	I
P	B	W	C	N	E	R	K	R	K	S
S	U	O	E	T	R	U	O	C	E	P
R	S	Z	P	D	X	S	L	U	A	U
A	Y	P	N	R	L	C	V	E	I	T
P	E	R	T	I	L	E	K	P	O	E
C	O	N	S	I	D	E	R	A	T	E
G	B	F	L	O	N	E	L	Y	T	R

Name _____

Word Box kind cooperative share courteous dispute lonely considerate loyal

Fill-in-the-Blank Crossword

Across

2. Dogs are known for being very _____ pets.

3. Ben is _____ and works well with his project group.

5. The team members got into a _____ over mistakes and delays.

7. Please be _____ and lower your voices in the library.

Down

1. Peter was _____ to his little brother because he cared about him.

2. When I first moved to a new city, I felt a little _____.

4. It is _____ to hold a door open for the person behind you.

6. Jose was nice to _____ his computer with Kevin.

Pickle-ade

CHARACTERS

Narrator	Chris	Group (role for 2
Billy	Mrs. Marks	or more)
Neighbor	The Mayor	

Narrator: Billy lived in the town of Pleasantville. Every summer, he sold lemonade at a stand in front of his house.

Billy: I'm tired of lemonade. Nobody in Pleasantville ever tries anything new. I want to make a different kind of drink.

Narrator: Billy looked in the refrigerator. Hmm. . . a jar of pickles. He poured the pickle juice into a pitcher and added a cup of sugar. This was a brand new drink. Billy tried it. He was surprised.

Billy: I can't believe it. This tastes really great!

Narrator:	Billy set up his stand. He made a sign that said "Pickle-ade." His next-door **neighbor** was the first to stop by.

> **neighbor** (*noun*, nay-bur): a person who lives close by

Neighbor:	What is this strange green drink?
Billy:	Pickle-ade. It is 50 cents a cup.
Neighbor:	Pickle-ade! No thank you! I don't like to try new things.
Billy:	That's too bad. I think you would like it.
Narrator:	Billy waited. Soon he saw a **pedestrian** walking down the street toward him. When the person got closer, Billy saw that it was his friend, Chris.

> **pedestrian** (*noun*, puh-dess-tree-uhn): a person who is walking

Billy:	Can I offer you a cup of pickle-ade?
Chris:	Pickle-ade! No way! I want to have the same drink I always have.
Billy:	That's too bad. I think you would like it.
Narrator:	This was not going well. Nobody wanted to try Billy's pickle-ade. Then a woman he had never seen before stopped at his stand.
Mrs. Marks:	Hello. I am from Trytown, the next town over. I am a **volunteer.** I am visiting your town to help plant a garden.

> **volunteer** (*noun*, vol-uhn-tihr): a person who offers to work or help without pay

Billy:	Can I offer you a cup of pickle-ade?
Volunteer:	Sure. I'd be happy to try it.
Narrator:	Mrs. Marks took a small sip of pickle-ade. She took another sip. She drank down the whole the cup.

Mrs. Marks: This tastes great! I'll have another pickle-ade, please. I can't wait to tell everyone about this.

Billy: Wow! She really likes my pickle-ade.

Narrator: Billy waited at his stand. Soon he saw a big group of pedestrians **strolling** down his street. Mrs. Marks was leading them.

---

stroll (*verb*, strohl): to walk slowly in a relaxed manner

Mrs. Marks: You have to try this pickle-ade. It is so tasty.

Narrator: Each one bought a cup of pickle-ade.

Group (*together*): You are right. This is great! This is the best drink ever!

Narrator: Billy's neighbor overheard the happy people talking. Now the neighbor wanted to try it.

Neighbor: This is amazing!

Narrator: Billy's friend Chris came back. Now Chris wanted to try pickle-ade.

Chris: I love it!

Narrator: People kept coming. Some people even came in their cars. Soon there was a line of **traffic** down Billy's street. Everyone wanted pickle-ade.

---

traffic (*noun*, traf-ik): All the cars, trucks, and buses moving along a road or street

---

Billy: I invented a new drink. It's a hit. The whole **community** loves it.

---

community (*noun*, kuh-myoo-nuh-tee): a group of people that live together in a neighborhood, town, or city

---

Narrator:	A man stopped at Billy's stand. The man was wearing a suit and a hat.
Billy:	Would you like a cup of pickle-ade?
The Mayor:	Yes, I would. I am the **mayor**. I have heard all about pickle-ade.

> **mayor** (*noun*, may-ur): the elected head of a town or city

Billy:	Here you are, mayor.
Narrator:	The mayor held up his cup. He took a small sip. He took another. He took a big gulp. Everyone cheered.
The Mayor:	This pickle-ade is great!
Billy:	I'm glad you like it.
The Mayor:	Life here in Pleasantville is very pleasant, but sometimes it gets a bit dull. Billy got people to try something new. Thank you, Billy. We are going to put up a **statue** of you in the park.

> **statue** (*noun*, stach-oo): a piece of art that is shaped out of stone, metal, or other material. Statues are often in the form of a human or animal.

Narrator:	A month later, Billy visited the park. There was a big statue of him. He couldn't believe it. The next summer, he made onion-ade. Everyone in Pleasantville tried some. Guess what? His neighbors loved it. Even Billy was surprised.

Word Challenge

Here are three more words having to do with neighborhoods.
Can you use each word in a sentence?

avenue (*noun*, av-uh-noo): a wide street often lined with trees

civic (*adj.*, siv-ik): related to a town or city

vehicle (*noun*, vee-uh-kuhl): a car, truck, or other type of land transportation

Name _____

Word Box neighbor pedestrian volunteer stroll traffic community mayor statue

Word Jumble

The letters of these vocabulary words are all mixed up. Using the word box above, figure out the correct answer and write it on the blank provided.

1. t c i r f f a _____ meaning: *all the vehicles moving along a road or street*

2. v l e r u t e n o _____ meaning: *a person who helps with a task without getting paid*

3. s t u e t a _____ meaning: *a sculpture of a person or animal*

4. c u n i o m t y m _____ meaning: *a group of people that live together in a neighborhood, town, or city*

5. o r n g h b e i _____ meaning: *a person who lives close by to where you live*

6. p e r i a n s t e d _____ meaning: *a person who is walking*

7. m y o r a _____ meaning: *the elected head of a town or city*

8. r l o l t s _____ meaning: *to walk in a relaxed manner*

Word Search

Using the word box above, can you find and circle the vocabulary words found from this unit?

L	L	O	R	T	S	T	S	P	R	S
L	E	V	O	L	U	N	T	E	E	R
H	U	B	I	D	S	P	E	D	Q	E
S	T	A	T	U	E	X	M	E	P	L
B	N	G	P	O	E	A	S	S	X	T
I	T	A	C	V	R	P	Q	T	A	M
Z	K	I	O	R	N	A	D	R	G	A
Z	L	C	O	M	M	U	N	I	T	Y
T	R	A	F	F	I	C	J	A	T	O
E	J	E	I	P	L	J	L	N	R	R
N	E	I	G	H	B	O	R	O	B	E

Name _____

Word Box neighbor   pedestrian   volunteer   stroll   traffic   community   mayor   statue

Fill-in-the-Blank Crossword

Across

2. There is a life-sized _____ in the park of George Washington.

3. Pedro's mother is a _____ at his school. She reads to the kindergarteners.

6. Our school works hard to be a kind and caring _____ of learners.

8. Our _____ lives next door and has a nice dog we like to pet!

Down

1. If you ride your bike on the sidewalk, you could hit a _____.

4. There was _____ on the highway because of a car accident.

5. Let's _____ along the beach and collect shells.

7. The town has elected a new _____.

Big Happy Family

CHARACTERS

Narrator	Mom	Cousin Pat
Dad	Grandfather	Little Brother
Julia	Aunt Sally	

Narrator: It was Julia's family **reunion**. People from her family were visiting from all over the country.

reunion (*noun*, ree-yoon-yuhn): a gathering of family or friends who have been apart from each other

Dad: This is going to be a great family reunion.

Mom: It sure is. Aren't you happy, Julia?

Julia: Sure. I guess so.

Narrator: Julia was happy. But she also felt a little scared. There was going to be a talent show at the family reunion. Everyone would do something special.

Julia:	What should I do at the show?
Mom:	I don't know. It can be anything you want. I'm sure you will do great.
Narrator:	The show started. The first person on the stage was Julia's **grandfather**.

grandfather (*noun*, grand-fah-thur): the father of your mother or father

Grandfather:	I have an apple. I also have a ball and a spoon. Now watch this.
Narrator:	Julia's grandfather juggled.
Everyone:	Yay!
Narrator:	Next it was Sally's turn. Sally was Julia's **aunt**.

aunt (*noun*, ant or ahnt): the sister of your mother or father

Aunt Sally:	I made up a song just for the reunion. Here it goes.
Narrator:	Aunt Sally started to sing.
Aunt Sally (*singing*):	We are a family. We have a big family tree. We are all so happy. Everyone, please sing along.
Everyone (*singing*):	We are a family. We have a big family tree. We are all so happy.
Narrator:	Then it was Pat's turn. Pat was Julia's **cousin**. Pat did a magic trick.

cousin (*noun*, kuhz-uhn): the child of your uncle or aunt

Cousin Pat:	Will someone please say a number from one to ten.
Grandfather:	Three!
Cousin Pat:	Now I will just lift this napkin. Look. There are three forks under it.

Everyone:	Wow!
Narrator:	Julia's dad told a funny story. Julia's mom read a poem. Soon almost all the **relatives** had done something. The only people left were Julia and her little brother.

> **relative** (*noun*, rel-uh-tiv): a person who belongs to the same family as someone else

Grandfather:	Whose turn is it now?
Aunt Sally:	I think it is the little one's turn.
Grandfather:	What does the **toddler** plan to do?

> **toddler** (*noun*, tod-lur): a young child who is just starting to walk

Little Brother:	Look at me! Look at me!
Grandfather:	I think he just put on his show.
Aunt Sally:	Yes, his special skill is being cute.
Everyone:	Yay.
Narrator:	Even Julia's little brother had done something. Julia was the only one left. Now it was her turn.
Grandfather:	What will you do Julia?
Cousin Pat:	Yes, we have been looking forward to your show.
Narrator:	Julia still wasn't sure. She knew she had to think fast.
Julia:	Okay, watch this.
Narrator:	Julia stood on her hands. Her little brother walked over. He tried to stand on his hands, too.

© 2013 Scholastic Inc. • *Perfect Plays for Building Vocabulary, Grades 3–4*

Little Brother: Look at me! Look at me!

Narrator: Julia was a little upset. He'd had his turn. Then a funny thing happened. All the relatives stood on their hands, too.

Dad: Hey, let's sing our new song.

Narrator: All the relatives began to sing Aunt Sally's song. They sang while still standing on their hands.

Everyone (*singing*): We are a family. We have a big family tree. We are all so happy.

Narrator: All the singing was very **festive**.

festive (*adj.*, fess-tiv): cheerful and fitting for a celebration

Grandfather: Good job, Julia. I have not stood on my hands in years. This sure is fun.

Mom: Now we have a new family **tradition**. We will have to do this at every reunion.

tradition (*noun*, truh-dish-uhn): an activity or custom that is done again and again over time

Narrator: Julia kept standing on her hands. Now she had a big smile.

Word Challenge

Here are three more words having to do with family.
Can you use each word in a sentence?

ancestor (*noun*, an-sess-tur): a person, often from long ago, that one is related to

infant (*noun*, in-fuhnt): a baby

sibling (*noun*, sib-ling): a brother or sister

Name _____

Word Box reunion grandfather aunt cousin relative toddler festive tradition

Word Jumble

The letters of these vocabulary words are all mixed up. Using the word box above, figure out the correct answer and write it on the blank provided.

1. r i o n a t d i t _____ meaning: *a custom that is done again and again over time*

2. s o u i n c _____ meaning: *the child of your uncle or aunt*

3. r h g r e f a n d a t _____ meaning: *the father of your mother or father*

4. u n n i o r e _____ meaning: *a gathering of family members*

5. r l e e a t v i _____ meaning: *a person that is part of your extended family*

6. a t u n _____ meaning: *the sister of your mother or father*

7. f t i e v e s _____ meaning: *fitting for a celebration*

8. d d l t o r e _____ meaning: *a young child*

Word Search

Using the word box above, can you find and circle the vocabulary words found from this unit?

E	V	I	T	A	L	E	R	F	A	M
X	L	I	V	U	W	G	U	O	E	N
L	S	A	C	O	U	S	I	N	R	O
A	T	I	U	U	M	D	F	G	P	I
P	B	O	A	N	E	R	Y	B	J	N
T	R	A	D	I	T	I	O	N	L	U
R	S	O	P	D	I	S	D	U	A	E
A	Y	P	N	R	L	N	V	E	I	R
F	E	S	T	I	V	E	J	P	O	H
O	L	N	Q	I	S	N	R	D	N	S
G	R	A	N	D	F	A	T	H	E	R

Name _____

Word Box reunion grandfather aunt cousin relative toddler festive tradition

Fill-in-the-Blank Crossword

Across

1. Sophie's _____ is 80 years old.

5. The mood at the party was _____.

6. Isabelle is excited because her _____ and uncle are visiting.

7. All the family members came to the _____. It was a wonderful picnic.

8. A _____ is a young child who is just learning to walk.

Down

2. Thanksgiving dinner is an American _____.

3. My aunt and uncle are having a baby. He will be my _____.

4. A brother is a _____ and so is a cousin or a grandmother or an uncle.

The Super-Cool Size Machine

CHARACTERS

Narrator	Anna	Big Baby
Barker	Ethan	Townspeople
Luke	Brooke	

Narrator: Middletown was having a fair. There were all kinds of fun and games. There was ring toss. There were pony rides. There was also something called the Super-Cool Size Machine.

Barker: Step right up. Try out the size machine. It only costs one dollar! Visit Big Land. See small things turned large! Visit Small Land. See **humongous** things turned teeny, tiny!

humongous (*adj.*, hyoo-muhng-guhs): very large in size

Luke:	That sounds really cool. Let's try it.
Narrator:	The kids paid one dollar each. They got in the Super-Cool Size Machine. It made lots of sounds. The door opened and the four kids went out.
Anna:	Wow! Everything here is so big.
Ethan:	Look at that. It is a huge baby bottle full of milk. It is as tall as a house.
Brooke:	Look over there. That's a big rattle. It is the **length** of a bus!

length (*noun*, lengkth): the distance from one end of a thing to the other

Narrator:	Something flew over the kids' heads. It looked like a big bird.
Luke:	What was that?
Anna:	It is a **gigantic** fly! Can you believe it?

gigantic (*adj.*, jahy-gan-tik): of very great size

Narrator:	Then a loud sound started. It went clump, clump, clump. The floor shook.
Ethan:	Something is coming.
Brooke:	Something really big is coming. Do you think it is an elephant? Do you think it might be a giant?
Luke:	No. It is a baby. It is a **massive** baby!

massive (*adj.*, mass-iv): very large and very heavy

Narrator:	Clump, clump, clump. The massive baby crawled across the floor. The baby made a funny face and then…
Big Baby:	BURP!!!
Anna:	That burp was so loud. That is one big baby!

Ethan: Babies put small things in their mouths. We are small things. Let's get out of here!

Narrator: The kids ran back to the size machine. They jumped inside and closed the door. The machine made lots of sounds. The doors opened and the kids got out.

Brooke: This is strange. We are standing in a puddle.

Luke: What are all these puffy things by our heads? They look like little pieces of cotton.

Anna: Let's get out of this puddle. Let's walk over that way.

Narrator: The kids walked toward the dry ground. They were about to step onto it. Then they saw something.

Ethan: Be careful! Don't step there. It is a **miniscule** town.

> **minuscule** (*adj.*, min-uh-skyool): extremely small or tiny

Brooke: I can't believe it! Look at all those **miniature** buildings. Look at all those miniature cars. Look over there. It's a miniature park.

> **miniature** (*adj.*, min-ee-uh-cher): of smaller size than normal; often used to describe a small version of something

Luke: Shh! Everybody be quiet. I think I hear something. It sounds like tiny voices.

Narrator: The kids stood very still. They were very quiet.

Townspeople: Four giants just walked across the ocean. They are so tall that their heads are up in the clouds. They're going to step on us. Help!

Anna: This puddle we are standing in is a whole ocean! These puffy things by our heads are clouds! There's a whole town the size of a board game!

Ethan: I thought Big Land was scary. But I don't like Small Land. We look like giants to these tiny people. We're scaring *them*.

Brooke: Let's get out of here.

Narrator: The kids walked back to the size machine. They were careful to stay in the puddle. They got inside the machine and closed the door. It made lots of sounds. The doors opened and the kids were back at the fair.

Luke: Look. No more **colossal** babies.

> **colossal** (*adj.*, kuh-loss-uhl): extremely large

Anna: No more tiny people.

Ethan: Everyone is the right **height**. Everything is the right height.

> **height** (*noun*, hite): the distance from the bottom to the top

Brooke: Boy, I sure am glad to be back in Middletown.

Word Challenge

Here are three more words having to do with size.
Can you use each word in a sentence?

gargantuan (*adj.*, gahr-gan-choo-uhn): huge

immense (*adj.*, ih-mens): very big

microscopic (*adj.*, mahy-kruh-skop-ik): too small to be seen with human eyes; only visible using a microscope

Name _____

Word Box humongous length gigantic massive minuscule miniature colossal height

Word Jumble

The letters of these vocabulary words are all mixed up. Using the word box above, figure out the correct answer and write it on the blank provided.

1. l n h g t e _____ meaning: *the distance from one end to the other*

2. h i g t h e _____ meaning: *distance from bottom to top*

3. u m h o o u s n g _____ meaning: *extremely large, like an elephant*

4. s m i l e n u c u _____ meaning: *extremely tiny*

5. s i v e m a s _____ meaning: *very large and heavy*

6. c l o s l s a o _____ meaning: *very large, especially a building*

7. a t m u e r i i n _____ meaning: *a smaller version of an original*

8. g n t i c g i a _____ meaning: *very big, like a giant*

Word Search

Using the word box above, can you find and circle the vocabulary words found from this unit?

I	O	M	A	S	S	I	V	E	P	R
X	M	I	N	U	S	C	U	L	E	R
L	S	N	U	L	E	N	G	T	H	S
A	U	I	R	U	E	D	M	E	P	V
S	O	A	C	E	E	A	A	S	J	O
T	M	T	C	O	L	O	S	S	A	L
H	C	U	N	R	I	I	D	R	A	K
G	Y	R	C	I	T	N	A	G	I	G
I	Z	E	R	F	L	C	J	N	O	R
E	O	N	Q	I	E	E	N	C	T	Y
H	U	M	O	N	G	O	U	S	M	D

Name _____

Word Box humongous   length   gigantic   massive   minuscule   miniature   colossal   height

Fill-in-the-Blank Crossword

Across

1. The toddler was half the _____ of her older sister.

3. The mountain was so _____, it was unlikely a tunnel could be drilled through it.

5. The new football stadium is _____.

7. The _____ furniture was perfect for the dollhouse.

Down

2. Wow, that whale is _____.

3. A grain of sand is _____.

4. That's a _____ hamburger.

6. The _____ of the cat's tail is ten inches.

How Did It Make You Feel?

CHARACTERS

Miss Harris	Jada	Nick	Class
Miguel	Sean	Emily	
Amber	Pat	Jordan	

Miss Harris: Okay, class. Today, we're going to talk about feelings. I'll ask a question. Raise your hand and tell me if it has ever happened to you. And tell me how it made you feel.

Here is the first question. Has anyone in this class ever been caught in a big rain?

Miguel (*raising hand*): I have. My clothes were all wet. Even my shoes and socks were wet.

Miss Harris: How did it make you feel?

Miguel: I felt **miserable**.

> **miserable** (*adj.*, miz-ur-uh-buhl): very unhappy or very uncomfortable

Miss Harris: Good, Miguel. I have also been caught in the rain. It made me feel miserable, too. Now, has anyone ever petted a puppy or kitten?

Amber: I have a little kitten. She is gray with white spots on her feet. Her name is Socks. I love to pet her.

Miss Harris: How does petting Socks make you feel?

Amber: It makes me feel happy.

Miss Harris: Good answer, Amber. Now, has anyone ever done really well at a sport?

Jada (*raising hand*): I play soccer. I scored three goals in one game.

Miss Harris: That's great, Jada. How did that make you feel?

Jada: It gave me lots of **confidence**.

> **confidence** (*noun*, kon-fi-duhns): a sense of trust or faith in a person or thing, or in oneself

Miss Harris: Good, Jada. Okay, class. Has anyone here ever known someone who was better at something?

Sean: My sister is a really good singer. She's the best singer in my family.

Miss Harris: How does that make you feel?

Sean: I'm **jealous** of my sister. I wish I could sing as well as she does.

> **jealous** (*adj.*, jel-uhs): Wishing to have another person's skills or possessions

Miss Harris: I wish I could sing, too. I'm jealous of people who sing really well. Now, who in this class has ever done something really hard?

Pat: I read a really long book. I did not think I could read it all. It was 300 pages long! But I read the whole thing.

Miss Harris: How did that make you feel?

Pat: I felt really **proud**. It was a big book!

> **proud** (*adj.*, prowd): to feel happy about your own achievements or those of someone else

Miss Harris: Good job, Pat. You should feel proud. Okay, kids. Has anyone here ever not gotten a good night's sleep?

Nick: One time I could not sleep. I stayed awake until very late. The next day in class I could not keep my eyes open.

Miss Harris: How did you feel?

Nick: I felt tired and I felt **grumpy**.

> **grumpy** (*adj.*, gruhm-pee): cranky and bad tempered

Miss Harris: Good answer, Nick. I also feel grumpy when I don't get enough sleep. Now, who here has stayed inside on a very cold day?

Emily: I have. I got under a blanket and had a bowl of hot soup.

Miss Harris: How did you feel?

Emily: I felt **cozy**.

> **cozy** (*adj.*, koh-zee): a feeling of comfort, warmth, and relaxation

© 2013 Scholastic Inc • *Perfect Plays for Building Vocabulary, Grades 3–4*

Miss Harris: That sounds cozy, Emily. Okay, who here has ever made a silly mistake?

Jordan: I went to a party. I thought the other kids were going to dress up. I wore a mask. Nobody else did.

Miss Harris: How did you feel?

Jordan: I was **embarrassed**.

embarrassed (*adj.*, em-bare-uhst): to feel awkward or ashamed

Miss Harris: Good answer, Jordan. I bet everything was fine when you took off the mask.

Thank you everyone for sharing your feelings. Are you ready to feel a new **emotion**? Guess what? I brought cupcakes for everyone. How does that make you feel?

emotion (*noun*, ih-moh-shuhn): a mood or feeling, such as joy or sadness

Class: Great! Happy! Hungry! Excited!

Word Challenge

Here are three more words having to do with feelings.
Can you use each word in a sentence?

baffled (*adj.*, baf-uhld): confused

delighted (*adj.*, di-lie-tid): feeling great happiness

glum (*adj.*, gluhm): sad

Name _____

Word Jumble

The letters of these vocabulary words are all mixed up. Using the word box above, figure out the correct answer and write it on the blank provided.

1. **c n c e d e f i o n** _____ meaning: *a feeling of sureness about one's own skills*

2. **y u m g r p** _____ meaning: *cranky and bad tempered*

3. **b a d s e e r a s r m** _____ meaning: *to feel awkward or ashamed*

4. **m e b l e r a i s** _____ meaning: *very unhappy or uncomfortable*

5. **d o p r u** _____ meaning: *to feel happy about your own achievements or those of someone else*

6. **e l o u s j a** _____ meaning: *wishing to have what someone else has*

7. **z y c o** _____ meaning: *a feeling of comfort and warmth*

8. **e o n o t i m** _____ meaning: *a feeling, such as joy or sadness*

Word Search

Using the word box above, can you find and circle the vocabulary words found from this unit?

E	M	B	A	R	R	A	S	S	E	D
M	M	L	O	R	U	N	T	E	E	R
O	S	B	U	J	E	A	L	O	U	S
T	U	N	A	U	E	D	M	E	P	P
I	O	R	C	R	E	A	A	S	K	R
O	M	I	S	E	R	A	B	L	E	O
N	C	T	O	R	N	A	D	R	A	U
Z	Y	C	G	W	M	U	S	V	H	D
T	Z	O	F	F	I	C	J	S	O	R
C	O	N	F	I	D	E	N	C	E	Y
Q	C	Y	P	M	U	R	G	O	S	D

Name _____

Word Box miserable confidence jealous proud grumpy cozy embarrassed emotion

Fill-in-the-Blank Crossword

Across

3. Sadness is an _____ that no one enjoys.

5. Gary has a cold and fever and feels _____.

6. Sara plays piano well and that makes Sal _____.

7. Scoring two goals in soccer gave Ann lots of _____ in her ability.

Down

1. Doing well on the math test makes Juan _____.

2. It feels _____ to sit near a fireplace.

3. Tina was _____ when she dropped her tray in the lunchroom.

4. I feel _____ when I don't get enough sleep.

Name _____

Synonym Match

Draw a line from each vocabulary word to the word with a similar meaning.

1. snug	**confidence**
2. extremely unhappy	**grumpy**
3. pleased	**miserable**
4. envious	**cozy**
5. humiliated	**proud**
6. belief in oneself	**embarrassed**
7. grouchy	**jealous**
8. feeling	**emotion**

Find the Antonym

For each vocabulary word, circle the choice that is *most opposite* in meaning.

1. confidence	sweat	cheerfulness	self-doubt	nervousness
2. grumpy	sad	cheerful	funny	dim
3. emotion	lack of feeling	cold	sharp	inconsiderate
4. cozy	warm	uncomfortable	soft	friendly
5. proud	vain	smart	ignorant	ashamed
6. miserable	delighted	young	funny	stubborn
7. embarrassed	silly	angry	thrilled	insane
8. jealous	pleased	unhappy	smooth	dark

Dodge Ball

CHARACTERS

Announcer   White Knight (*Team Good Guy*)
Referee   Monster (*Team Bad Guy*)
Dragon (*Team Bad Guy*)   Unicorn (*Team Good Guy*)
Princess (*Team Good Guy*)   Dark Knight (*Team Bad Guy*)

Announcer: Hello sports fans! It is time for the Enchanted Forest dodge ball championship. It is Team Good Guy against Team Bad Guy.

Referee: Let's get this game started. Here are the rules. If the ball hits you, you are out of the game.

Team Bad Guy: Bring it on, heroes!

Team Good Guy: Get ready to lose, **villains**!

villain (*noun*, vil-uhn): an evil person or criminal

Announcer: The white knight throws a ball at the dragon. The dragon blows fire out of its nose. The fire melts the dodge ball.

Dragon: You cannot get me out of this game. I will melt every ball you throw at me.

Announcer: Now the dragon is going to throw the ball. The dragon is looking at the princess.

Princess: I must be **courageous**. I can dodge the ball at the last second.

courageous (*adj.*, kuh-ray-juhs): brave, not afraid of danger

Announcer: The dragon hits the ball with its tail. The ball goes very fast. It goes so fast that the princess cannot get out of the way.

White Knight: Don't fear, I will **rescue** you!

rescue (*verb*, ress-kyoo): to free or save someone

Announcer: The white knight jumps in front of the princess. He puts out his shield. The ball bounces off the shield. Look! The ball bounced back at the dragon. It hit the dragon before he could blow fire.

Referee: You are out of the game, Dragon.

Monster: You may have gotten the dragon out. But we will still win.

Announcer: The monster looks **evil**. He has four arms, and each arm is holding a dodge ball. Wait, he's throwing them all at the unicorn.

evil (*adj.*, ee-vuhl): very wrong or bad; wicked

Monster: Take that and that and that and that!

Unicorn: Four dodge balls at once! Oh no!

Announcer: The unicorn jumps over the first ball. He ducks another ball. He twists away from the third ball. Oh no, the fourth ball has hit the unicorn.

Referee: Unicorn, you're out of the game!

© 2013 Scholastic Inc • *Perfect Plays for Building Vocabulary, Grades 3–4*

Announcer:	The monster has been busy throwing all those dodge balls. He does not see the princess sneaking up behind him. Wait, she's throwing one.
Princess:	Take that, you **vile** monster!

> **vile** (*adj.*, vahyl): extremely bad, disgusting, or unpleasant

Referee:	You are out of the game, Monster.
Announcer:	Now, the dark knight throws a ball high into the air. The princess is looking at the ball. The dark knight rolls a second ball on the ground.
White Knight:	Look down!
Announcer:	The princess sees the ball high in the air. She does not see the ball on the ground. It rolls over and taps her foot.
Referee:	You are out of the game, Princess.
Announcer:	There are only two players left. There is one player from each team. It is the white knight against the dark knight. Who will win?
Dark Knight:	Ha-ha. I have many more tricks. Team Bad Guy will win this dodge ball game!
White Knight:	I will not use tricks. I will play with **honor**. Team Good Guy will win the dodge ball championship!

> **honor** (*noun*, on-ur): the state of having good character and honest behavior

Announcer:	The white knight is picking up a ball. The dark knight picks up a ball.
Dark Knight:	Hey, White Knight. Look over there!
White Knight:	I will not look over there.
Dark Knight:	Hey, White Knight. Your shoe is untied.

White Knight:	I am wearing metal shoes. They do not have strings.
Dark Knight:	Hey, White Knight. Check your watch. Can you tell me what time it is?
White Knight:	Don't worry, Dark Night. I'm about to show you what time it is!
Announcer:	The white knight runs at the dark knight. The dark knight runs away like a **coward**. The white knight throws the ball.

> **coward** (*noun*, kow-erd): a person who does not have the courage to face danger, pain, or something difficult

White Knight:	You wanted to know the time. It's time for you to lose!
Announcer:	The ball hits the dark knight.
Referee:	You are out, Dark Knight. The game is over. Team Good Guy wins.
Princess:	You showed such **bravery**, White Knight. You are my hero.

> **bravery** (*noun*, brey-vuh-ree): the condition of not giving in to fear; courage

White Knight:	Thank you, my lady. I knew we could beat the bad guys.
Announcer:	This has been a great game. Tune in next week. We will have a softball game between elves and fairies.

Word Challenge

Here are three more words having to do with heroes and villains.
Can you use each word in a sentence?

loathsome (*adj.*, lohth-suhm): causing disgust or strong dislike

scoundrel (*noun*, skoun-druhl): a bad or dishonest person

virtuous (*adj.*, vur-choo-uhs): showing very good behavior

© 2013 Scholastic Inc • *Perfect Plays for Building Vocabulary, Grades 3–4*

Name _____

Word Box   villain   courageous   rescue   evil   vile   honor   coward   bravery

Word Jumble

The letters of these vocabulary words are all mixed up. Using the word box above, figure out the correct answer and write it on the blank provided.

1. l e i v _____ meaning: *disgusting and unpleasant*

2. e e u s c r _____ meaning: *to save someone from danger*

3. l a l i n v i _____ meaning: *an evil person*

4. w r o d c a _____ meaning: *someone easily scared or unable to face pain*

5. s u c o r g u a e o _____ meaning: *brave*

6. y r b v e r a _____ meaning: *behavior that shows courage*

7. r o h o n _____ meaning: *of good character*

8. e l i v _____ meaning: *wicked*

Word Search

Using the word box above, can you find and circle the vocabulary words found from this unit?

V	I	L	E	J	S	I	V	E	P	C
X	M	I	V	U	C	G	U	L	E	O
L	S	N	I	L	A	N	G	R	H	U
A	U	I	L	U	M	D	M	E	P	R
P	B	R	A	V	E	R	Y	S	J	A
D	H	D	T	O	B	I	Q	C	K	G
R	C	O	N	R	I	I	D	U	A	E
A	Y	B	N	I	T	N	A	E	I	O
W	Z	E	R	O	L	C	J	N	O	U
O	L	N	Q	I	R	E	N	C	T	S
C	B	N	I	A	L	L	I	V	M	D

Name _____

Word Box villain courageous rescue evil vile honor coward bravery

Fill-in-the-Blank Crossword

Across

6. The movie starred a wonderful hero who defeated the evil _____.

7. Firefighters are trained to _____ people.

Down

1. Hang-gliding is a _____ thing to do.

2. When Adam climbed way up high to help the cat in the tree, his mom was impressed with his _____.

3. My cat hides under the bed during storms. He is a _____.

4. The spoiled milk tasted _____.

5. She would never cheat on a test because she has _____.

8. The _____ queen wanted to lock the prince in a dungeon.

Name _____

Word Box   villain   courageous   rescue   evil   vile   honor   coward   bravery

Synonym Match

Draw a line from each vocabulary word to its synonym.

1. save	**evil**
2. extremely bad	**rescue**
3. respect	**courageous**
4. disgusting	**villain**
5. fearlessness	**bravery**
6. one who is scared	**honor**
7. evildoer	**coward**
8. heroic	**vile**

Find the Antonym

For each vocabulary word, circle the choice that is *most opposite* in meaning.

1. **rescue**	desert	help	fight	love
2. **bravery**	anger	cheer	fearfulness	strength
3. **coward**	help	hero	child	clock
4. **villain**	good guy	bad guy	brute	criminal
5. **vile**	gross	scary	smelly	delicious
6. **honor**	power	disgrace	strength	stubbornness
7. **courageous**	laughter	humor	fearful	craziness
8. **evil**	good	bad	dark	dishonest

Super Three vs. Badman

CHARACTERS

Narrator   Stickum   Badman
Police Chief   Flex
Bolt   Citizen

Narrator: The Super Three fight crime. Bolt is very fast. Flex is very stretchy. Stickum is very sticky.

Police Chief: We need your help, Super Three. Badman is back. He is playing tricks on the people of Center City.

Bolt: What is Badman doing?

Police Chief: He has an ice gun. He is making the streets icy. He is causing cars to **skid** all over the place.

---

skid (*verb*, skid): to slide, especially on slippery ground

© 2013 Scholastic Inc • *Perfect Plays for Building Vocabulary, Grades 3–4*

Bolt: Don't worry, Chief.

Stickum: We will stop Badman.

Flex: Okay, Super Three. Let's **spring** into action.

> **spring** (*verb*, spring): to jump or move suddenly upward or forward

Narrator: Flex stretches out like a long spring. Bolt begins running very fast. Stickum puts on his glue gloves. The Super Three are ready.

Citizen: Badman is over there. You have to stop him.

Bolt: I see Badman. I'll run fast and catch him.

Flex: Be careful. Badman is holding his ice gun.

Badman: Tee-hee. It is your lucky day, Bolt. You are about to become very cool.

Narrator: Badman shoots Bolt with an ice ray. Bolt runs slower and slower.

Stickum: Why is Bolt so **sluggish**?

> **sluggish** (*adj.*, sluhg-ish): slow moving and lacking energy

Flex: Badman's ice ray is slowing Bolt down. Oh no! Now Bolt is frozen in ice.

Badman: Tee-hee. Why is your name Bolt if you can't even move? Now watch as I make a **rapid** getaway.

> **rapid** (*adj.*, rap-id): happening quickly or in a short period of time

Flex: What is Badman doing now?

Stickum: He's getting into an airplane.

Flex: I have a plan to stop him.

Stickum: So do I.

Narrator: Badman **soars** up into the air in his plane. Flex stretches one arm chasing after Badman. Flex is trying to grab Badman's plane with the long arm.

soar (*verb*, sohr): to rise high into the air; to fly

Flex: If I can just reach my arm a little further. There, I've got you.

Narrator: Flex grabs the plane. Badman flies up. Badman flies down. Oh no! He has tied Flex's arm in a knot.

Flex: Ouch!

Badman: Flex, you are the best super hero… knot. Get it? Tee-hee. I tied your arm in a knot.

Narrator: Flex's arm hurts a lot. Flex lets go of the plane, and Badman flies away.

Narrator: Badman lands the plane. It looks like he has gotten away. But where is Stickum?

Stickum (*whispering*): Badman did not notice. I stuck myself to his plane. Now I will unstick myself and get him.

Narrator: Stickum **darts** out and grabs Badman as he gets out of the plane. Stickum puts glue on Badman's hands and sticks them behind his back. Then Stickum puts Badman back in the plane.

dart (*verb*, dahrt): to move quickly

Badman: Let me go! Let me go!

Stickum: Quiet down, Badman. You're in a lot of trouble.

Narrator: Stickum flies the plane back to Center City. Stickum unties Flex's arm and melts the ice from Bolt. The Super Three bring Badman to the police.

Police Chief: You caused trouble for the good people of this city. Now we are going to put a **halt** to your tricks.

halt (*noun*, hawlt): an end of something; a stop

Narrator: The Chief puts Badman in jail.

Stickum: Looks like you're *stuck* in jail, ha-ha.

Flex: You might want to *stretch* out on your bed. You'll be here for a while.

Bolt: Yes, time will not go **swiftly** for you.

swiftly (*adverb*, swift-lee): happening with great speed

Police Chief: You've put another bad guy behind bars. Good job, Super Three.

Word Challenge

Here are three more words having to do with movement.
Can you use each word in a sentence?

bound (*verb*, bound): to move in a leaping style

cling (*verb*, kling): to hold on tightly

lunge (*verb*, luhnj): to make a sudden forward movement

© 2013 Scholastic Inc • Perfect Plays for Building Vocabulary: Grades 3–4

Name _____

Word Jumble

The letters of these vocabulary words are all mixed up. Using the word box above, figure out the correct answer and write it on the blank provided.

1. g r i n s p _____ meaning: *to jump upward or forward*

2. s t l w i y f _____ meaning: *moving quickly*

3. g u s i h g s l _____ meaning: *slow moving*

4. a l t h _____ meaning: *an end or a stop*

5. a t r d _____ meaning: *to move quickly over a short distance*

6. k s i d _____ meaning: *to slide, especially on slippery ground*

7. s a r o _____ meaning: *to rise high into the air*

8. r p a d i _____ meaning: *very fast*

Word Search

Using the word box above, can you find and circle the vocabulary words found from this unit?

S	K	I	D	S	S	D	I	P	A	R
X	L	I	V	U	W	G	U	L	E	O
L	S	U	I	X	A	I	D	A	R	T
A	U	I	G	U	M	D	F	E	P	R
P	B	R	A	G	E	R	Y	T	J	G
D	V	S	O	O	I	I	Q	C	L	K
R	S	O	P	R	I	S	D	U	A	Y
A	Y	P	N	R	T	N	H	E	I	D
S	O	A	R	O	I	C	J	N	O	H
O	L	N	Q	I	S	N	I	D	T	S
C	H	A	L	T	L	L	G	V	M	T

Name _____

Word Box   skid   spring   sluggish   rapid   soar   dart   halt   swift

Fill-in-the-Blank Crossword

Across

2. The plane will _____ up into the sky.

3. Manny is feeling tired and _____ today.

5. The horse gallops at a _____ speed.

6. Did you see that deer _____ across the road?

Down

1. I saw the policeman _____ into action when the bank robber ran by.

2. The currents of the river are _____.

3. Jason stepped on the brakes and made his bike _____.

4. You must bring that bad behavior to a _____ immediately.

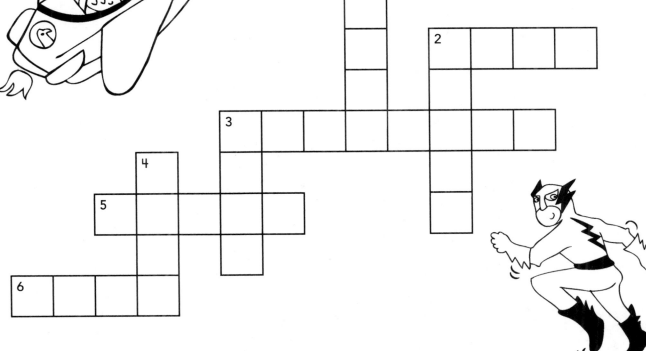

Robbie, the Nervous Weather Robot

CHARACTERS

Narrator	Tony	Sara
Liz	Robbie, the Robot	Marcus
Miles, science whiz	Emma	

Narrator: On the second day of third grade, Miles brought something amazing to school. It was a robot.

Liz: Did you make that robot by yourself?

Miles: Yes, I made him over summer break. He's a weather robot. His name is Robbie.

Liz: What does a weather robot do?

Miles: He can **forecast** the weather.

forecast (*verb*, fore-kast): to predict, especially about weather

Liz: Wow, how does he do that?

Miles: All you have to do is look outside and describe what you see to Robbie. He'll tell you what kind of weather is coming.

Tony: I want to try! I want to try!

Miles: Go ahead. Look out the window and just tell Robbie what you see.

Tony: Let's see. The wind is blowing and trees are swaying.

Robbie (*in robotic voice*): Alert! Alert! There is a **tornado** coming. Children, get under your desks.

> **tornado** (*noun*, tor-nayd-oh): a storm of very strong winds that form a cloud shaped like a funnel. Although it does not last long, a tornado can destroy everything in its path.

Miles: I think I had better fiddle with Robbie's controls.

Robbie: Reset! Reset! I made a mistake. Children, you can come out from under your desks now. Expect a very pleasant fall day with some **gusts** of wind.

> **gust** (*noun*, gust): a sudden rush or blast of wind

All kids: Hooray for fall! Hooray, Robbie!

Robbie (*in robotic voice*): Thank you!

Narrator: Miles kept bringing Robbie the Robot to school every day. Soon the autumn was over and winter began. The weather was changing.

Emma: Look outside. The sky is turning gray.

Miles: Tell Robbie. He can make another weather forecast.

Emma: Robbie, it is getting colder outside, and the sky is pale and gray. What kind of weather are we going to get?

Robbie: Alert! Alert! There is a **blizzard** coming! Children, put on your coats and mittens and huddle together to stay warm.

> **blizzard** (*noun*, bli-zard): a severe snowstorm with high winds that lasts a long time

Miles:	That doesn't sound right. I guess I need to fiddle with Robbie's controls some more.
Robbie:	Reset! Reset! Beep! Beep! A mistake was made. Children, please take off your mittens. Expect the weather to be partly cloudy today with light snow.
All kids:	Hooray for winter! Hooray, Robbie!
Robbie (*in robotic voice*): Thank you!	
Narrator:	Miles kept bringing Robbie to school each day. The weather kept changing. Soon it was spring.
Sara:	All the snow has melted. I even saw a baby robin on the way to school.
Miles:	Tell Robbie. Maybe he can make a forecast.
Sara:	The **temperature** outside is nice, Robbie. But it is just starting to rain.

temperature (*noun*, tem-puh-ruh-chuhr): the measurement of heat or cold as shown in degrees on a thermometer

Robbie:	Alert! Alert! There is a big storm coming. There will be loud thunder. Children, cover your ears!
Miles:	Not again! I'm going to have to keep fiddling with Robbie's controls until he works properly.
Robbie:	Reset! Reset! I made a mistake. Children, uncover your ears. Expect a spring day with light **drizzle** in the afternoon.

drizzle (*noun*, driz-uhl): a light, steady rain

All kids:	Hooray for spring! Hooray, Robbie!
Robbie (*in robotic voice*): Thank you!	

Narrator: The weather continued to change. Soon it was almost the end of the school year.

Marcus: It's starting to get hot. I was sweating at recess.

Miles: Tell Robbie. He can give us a new forecast.

Marcus: Today is really warm and sunny, Robbie. What do you think is going to happen?

Robbie: Alert! Alert! Today is **sweltering**! Children, you better stay inside during recess to avoid heat stroke!

sweltering (*adj.*, swel-tuhr-eng): overly hot or humid

Miles: I cannot figure out what's wrong with Robbie. I guess he's just nervous about the weather. Looks like I'll always have to keep fiddling with his controls.

Robbie: Reset! Reset! I made a mistake. Children, no need to water the flowers right now. Expect today to be sunny, warm, and a little **humid**.

humid (*adj.*, hyoo-mid): describes a time when there's a lot of moisture in the air

All kids: Hooray for summer! Hooray, Robbie!

Robbie (*in robotic voice*): Children, as soon as school is over, let's all head to the beach. Alert! Alert! Make sure to put on your sunscreen.

Word Challenge

Here are three more words having to do with weather.
Can you use each word in a sentence?

drought (*noun*, drout): a long period with little or no rain

frigid (*adj.*, frij-id): very cold

icicle (*noun*, ahy-si-kuhl): a long, hanging piece of ice

Name _____

> **Word Box** sweltering gust tornado temperature drizzle forecast humid blizzard

Word Jumble

The letters of these vocabulary words are all mixed up. Using the word box above, figure out the correct answer and write it on the blank provided.

1. l z d i a r z b _____ meaning: *a severe winter storm*

2. g s t u _____ meaning: *a strong burst of wind*

3. c t s e a f o r _____ meaning: *a prediction about future weather*

4. w s e g e r i n l t _____ meaning: *uncomfortably hot*

5. z e z i l d r _____ meaning: *a very light, misty rain*

6. t e r r e a u t e m p _____ meaning: *measurement of hot or cold*

7. h m i u d _____ meaning: *having heavy moisture in the air*

8. t a o d o r n _____ meaning: *a powerful storm with strong winds that spin in the shape of a funnel*

Word Search

Using the word box above, can you find and circle the vocabulary words found from this unit?

T	X	D	G	U	S	T	S	O	R	S
L	E	Q	J	N	C	I	X	A	N	W
H	U	M	I	D	S	P	E	N	W	E
D	O	Z	P	T	I	X	M	U	Y	L
R	F	O	R	E	C	A	S	T	R	T
I	Y	M	C	V	R	P	Q	I	D	E
Z	K	T	O	R	N	A	D	O	V	R
Z	L	N	B	T	I	L	T	M	E	I
L	Y	K	Q	O	A	N	J	U	T	N
E	J	E	I	P	X	J	L	W	R	G
B	L	I	Z	Z	A	R	D	O	B	E

Name _____

Word Box sweltering gust tornado temperature drizzle forecast humid blizzard

Fill-in-the-Blank Crossword

Across

3. A _____ of wind blew off people's hats.

6. During the _____, over three feet of snow fell.

7. The _____ today is just right—not too hot, not too cold.

8. A _____ is also called a twister.

Down

1. It is hot and _____ today.

2. In a light _____, it's good to have an umbrella.

4. The hottest summer days are _____.

5. Did you hear the weather _____ on the radio?

What's in the Woods?

CHARACTERS

Narrator	José	Campers
Jake, camp counselor	Timmy	Kim
Megan	Zoe	

Narrator: A group of kids was at Camp Deep Woods. The kids were sitting around a campfire. They were eating hot dogs and chips.

Jake: Okay, campers. Finish up your food. It is time to get in your tents. It is time to go to sleep.

Megan: What was that?

Jake: What?

Megan: I heard a sound.

Jake: It is night now. There are lots of animals in the woods. I bet the sound you heard was just a **nocturnal** animal.

nocturnal (*adj.*, nok-tur-nl): active at night or occurring during the night

© 2013 Scholastic Inc • *Perfect Plays for Building Vocabulary, Grades 3–4*

José: What kind of nocturnal animal? There must be all kinds of animals out in the woods at night.

Jake: I'm not sure what kind of animal. I did not hear the sound.

Other campers: We did. There's the sound again!

José: What if the animal is mean? What if it has sharp teeth and sharp claws? What if it is just waiting to **pounce**?

> **pounce** (*verb*, pouns): to jump quickly, or to spring in order to catch prey

Timmy: I'm scared. I want to go home.

Jake: There is nothing to be scared of. I'm sure it is not a mean animal.

Narrator: The campers sat in the dark near the fire. Jake's words helped. But now they were all a little scared.

Megan: What was that?

Jake: Now what?

Megan: I just saw something move. It is coming right toward us.

Jake: Don't worry, campers. I'm sure it's just a little animal. Let's not get all worked up.

Megan: It doesn't look small to me. I can see its shadow in the light of the fire.

Other campers: We see it, too. It looks **enormous**!

> **enormous** (*adj.*, ih-nawr-muhs): very large in size or quantity

Zoe: What if it's a bear or a wolf? Maybe it's a lion or tiger or some other **predator**.

> **predator** (*noun*, pred-uh-ter): an animal that hunts other animals for food

Timmy: I'm scared. I want my mommy!

Jake: I still don't see anything. Calm down, campers. None of those **species** of animals lives in these woods.

---

species (*noun*, spee-sheez): a group of animals that are similar

---

Narrator: Jake's words helped a little. But the campers were getting more and more scared.

Megan: Oh my! Now I see a pair of eyes. I'm sure there is an animal out there. It is staring right at us!

Jake: I see the eyes, too.

Other campers: Me, too!

Megan: What kind of animal is it?

Jake: I don't know.

José: What if it's a new type of animal that no one has ever seen before?

Kim: What if it's a scary animal that only comes out at night? What if it's **venomous**?

---

venomous (*adj.*, ven-uh-muhs): describes an animal that can inject venom (poison) through a bite or sting

---

Jake (*whispering*): Shh. There are no large predators in these woods. There are no venomous animals here, either. If we sit quietly, we may get to see a cool animal.

Narrator: The campers stared at the two eyes. The two **keen** eyes stared back at the campers.

---

keen (*adj.*, keen): able to notice things easily

© 2013 Scholastic Inc • *Perfect Plays for Building Vocabulary, Grades 3–4*

Timmy:	Mommy!
Jake:	Shhhh, Timmy. Don't worry. Whatever it is, it is a nice animal.
Narrator:	The campers saw the animal **scurry** toward them. They could not believe it! It was so small. It was so cute. It was a…

scurry (*verb*, skuh-ree): to move quickly with small steps

Other campers:	Chipmunk!
Narrator:	The little chipmunk picked up a chip. It started to munch on it. The campers watched the chipmunk eat.
Timmy:	Camping is great. I get to watch wild animals in the woods. I'm having a great time!
Other campers:	Me, too!

Word Challenge

Here are three more words having to do with animals.
Can you use each word in a sentence?

burrow (*verb*, bur-oh): to dig or make a hole

camouflage (*noun*, kam-uh-flahzh): colors and markings on an animal that allow it to blend in

migrate (*verb*, mahy-greyt): to move from one region to another, especially with the change of seasons

Name _____

Word Box nocturnal pounce enormous predator species venomous keen scurry

Word Jumble

The letters of these vocabulary words are all mixed up. Using the word box above, figure out the correct answer and write it on the blank provided.

1. e n e k _____ meaning: *very good sight or hearing*

2. o u n p e c _____ meaning: *to jump upon something quickly, such as prey*

3. n u a l r n o c t _____ meaning: *active at night*

4. o o u s r m e n _____ meaning: *very large*

5. v e n m o s u o _____ meaning: *a poisonous animal*

6. y r c u r s _____ meaning: *to move with small, quick steps*

7. i e s p e s c _____ meaning: *a group of animals with similar characteristics*

8. p o r d a r e t _____ meaning: *an animal that hunts other animals*

Word Search

Using the word box above, can you find and circle the vocabulary words found from this unit?

K	L	O	P	S	E	I	C	E	P	S
E	E	L	O	R	U	N	T	E	E	R
E	S	A	U	D	E	P	S	D	Q	E
N	U	N	N	U	E	D	M	E	P	U
B	O	R	C	O	E	A	A	S	X	S
I	M	U	E	V	R	P	Q	T	A	C
Z	R	T	O	N	R	A	D	R	O	U
Z	O	C	G	W	M	U	I	V	T	R
T	N	O	F	F	I	C	J	A	T	R
V	E	N	O	M	O	U	S	L	R	Y
Q	P	I	B	H	X	O	Z	O	B	E

© 2013 Scholastic Inc • *Perfect Plays for Building Vocabulary, Grades 3–4* • page 62

Name _____

Word Box nocturnal pounce enormous predator species venomous keen scurry

Fill-in-the-Blank Crossword

Across

1. The tiger is about to _____ on its prey.

3. Dogs and cats are different _____ of animals.

5. Be careful! That snake might be _____.

Down

1. A _____ is an animal that hunts other animals.

2. Eagles have _____ eyesight.

3. Did you see that mouse _____ across the room?

4. Bats are _____. They come out at night.

6. A whale is _____ in size.

A Monster Meal

CHARACTERS

Narrator
Og (monster)
Zop (monster)

Blug (monster)
Snork (monster)
Weef (monster)

Mr. Smithson
Mrs. Smithson

Narrator:	Five monsters lived in an old house. Mr. and Mrs. Smithson had just moved in next door. The monsters had invited their new neighbors over for dinner.
Og:	What do you think humans like to eat?
Zop:	I have heard they like soup.
Blug:	Good idea, Zop! Let's make soup!
Snork:	Yes, let's make soup. I love to cook.
Weef:	Yes, cooking for people will be fun. Don't forget to put on your **aprons**.

apron (*noun*, ey-pruhn): a garment that covers the front of the body to protect the clothing underneath

© 2013 Scholastic Inc • Perfect Plays for Building Vocabulary, Grades 3–4

Narrator:	The monsters put on their aprons. Each had something written on it. One said, "World's Best Monster Cook." Another said, "Hug a Monster."
Og:	Let's get started. I have filled this pot with water fresh from the pond.
Zop:	I will toss in some weeds. I picked them in our weed garden. Aren't they pretty? I've seen people eat plants. I think the Smithsons will like these.
Blug:	I will add this donut. I wear it as a ring. But I have heard that people eat donuts.
Snork:	I will add some toothpaste. I like to snack on toothpaste. I bet the Smithsons like it, too.
Og:	I have a secret **ingredient**.

ingredient (*noun*, in-gree-dee-uhnt): one part of a mixture, often in a recipe

Zop:	What is it?
Og:	Peanut butter. I use peanut butter to clean myself in the bath. But I have heard that people love to eat peanut butter.
Narrator:	The monsters stirred the pot. It was full of pond water. And weeds. And a donut. And toothpaste. And peanut butter. The monsters watched and waited.
Og:	I see little bubbles in the water.
Zop:	The bubbles are getting bigger.
Blug:	The pot is starting to **boil**.

boil (*verb*, boil): to heat a liquid until it is very hot and bubbly

All Monsters:	The Smithsons are going to love this soup!
Narrator:	Meanwhile, the Smithsons were making a dish to bring to the monsters.
Mr. Smithson:	What do you think monsters like to eat?

Mrs. Smithson: I looked in all my cookbooks. I could not find a **recipe** for monster meals. I think monsters like food that is messy and stinky and scary. Let's make a monster salad.

> **recipe** (*noun*, res-uh-pee): a list of ingredients and instructions for making a food

Mr. Smithson: Good idea. Let's fill this bowl with ketchup. That should be messy enough.

Mrs. Smithson: There is a piece of old cheese in the trash. It is starting to really stink. I will **grind** it up and put it in the salad.

> **grind** (*verb*, grynd): to crush something into small pieces

Mr. Smithson: I'll add some olives. They look kind of like eyeballs. That's scary.

Mrs. Smithson: Hmmm. I think this still needs something. How about just a **dash** of dirt.

> **dash** (*noun*, dash): a very small amount of something

Narrator: The Smithsons took a look at their dish. It was a bowl of ketchup. And some ground up old cheese. And olives. And a dash of dirt.

Mr. and Mrs. Smithson: The monsters are going to love this salad.

Narrator: The Smithsons went over to the monster house with their salad. The monsters were waiting with their soup. Everyone sat down for dinner.

Og: Thanks for being our guests. Let's dig in. **Bon appetit!**

> **bon appetit** (*interjection*, baw na-pey-tee): This is a French phrase that's now used in English. It means, "enjoy your meal."

Mr. Smithson (*taking a tiny spoonful*): This sure is tasty soup.

© 2013 Scholastic Inc. • *Perfect Plays for Building Vocabulary, Grades 3–4*

Mrs. Smithson (*trying hard not to make a face*): Why is that…toothpaste I taste? This is just yummy. You'll have to share your recipe with us.

Mr. and Mrs. Smithson (*whispering to each other*): What have these monsters made for us? This is bad. We can't eat this!

Zop (*taking a tiny forkful*): What a fine…salad.

Snork (*trying hard not to make a face*): The rotten cheese is a great touch.

All monsters (*whispering to each other*): What is this? What have these people made for us? It is not even **edible**.

> **edible** (*adj.*, ed-uh-buhl): able to be eaten; safe to eat

Narrator: The people could not eat the food the monsters had made. The monsters could not eat the food the people had made. This was turning out to be a very bad visit. But then Og the monster saved the day.

Og: I want to thank you, Mr. and Mrs. Smithson, for trying to make us salad. It was very thoughtful. But I have an idea. Why don't we just order pizza.

Mr. Smithson: Thank you so much, monsters, for trying to make us soup. That was also very thoughtful. Yes, what a great idea. Let's order pizza.

Everyone: People love pizza. Monsters love pizza. Everyone loves pizza!

Word Challenge

Here are three more words having to do with cooking.
Can you use each word in a sentence?

culinary (*adj.*, kuhl-uh-ner-ee): Related to cooking or cooking skills

scrumptious (*adj.*, skruhmp-shuhs): extremely tasty

season (*verb*, see-zuhn): to add spices to food

Name _____

> **Word Box**   apron   ingredient   grind   boil   dash   recipe   edible   bon appetit

Word Jumble

The letters of these vocabulary words are all mixed up. Using the word box above, figure out the correct answer and write it on the blank provided.

1. **s a h d** _____ meaning: *a very small amount of an ingredient, such as a spice*

2. **b e t i a p t p o n** _____ meaning: *a French phrase that means "enjoy your meal"*

3. **c i p e r e** _____ meaning: *a list of ingredients and instructions for making a specific food*

4. **d i b e l e** _____ meaning: *fit to be eaten*

5. **p a n o r** _____ meaning: *a piece of cloth worn to protect clothing*

6. **g r d i n** _____ meaning: *to crush into small pieces*

7. **l o b i** _____ meaning: *to heat a liquid until it boils*

8. **r d e i e n t g i n** _____ meaning: *one part of a mixture in a recipe*

Word Search

Using the word box above, can you find and circle the vocabulary words found from this unit?

I	M	B	T	R	E	P	I	C	E	R
M	N	L	O	R	U	N	T	E	E	R
D	S	G	U	G	R	I	N	D	U	S
A	U	N	R	U	E	D	M	E	P	B
S	O	R	C	E	E	A	A	S	J	O
H	M	I	S	E	D	I	B	L	E	I
N	C	T	N	R	I	I	D	R	A	L
Z	Y	C	O	W	B	U	E	V	L	D
T	Z	O	R	F	L	C	J	N	O	R
C	O	N	P	I	E	E	N	C	T	Y
B	O	N	A	P	P	E	T	I	T	D

Name _____

Word Box apron ingredient grind boil dash recipe edible bon appetit

Fill-in-the-Blank Crossword

Across

1. Some plants are _____, but some are not

6. Grandma wears an _____ when she bakes cookies.

7. The _____ for the cookies was easy to follow.

8. When water starts to _____, you can see little bubbles.

Down

2. This dish could use a _____ of salt.

3. "_____ _____!" said the waiter as he served our meal.

4. The coffee shop will _____ the coffee beans for you.

5. I forgot to add an important _____, and it ruined the recipe.

More Word Lists for 3rd and 4th Graders

Fairy tale words	myth • bold • treasure • triumph • envy • journey • heroic • humble • attractive • distress
Success words	industrious • impressive • ability • contribute • ambition • advice • attitude • competition • eager
Construction words	entrance • deed • excavate • survey • diagram • column • accurate
Geography words	arctic • continent • globe • nation • wander • resident • coast • border • atlas • peninsula
Conflict words	defend • fierce • terror • threat • valiant • captivity • furious • hardship
History words	ancient • civilization • passage • century • individual • privilege • symbol • noble • immigration
Medical words	disease • device • assist • prevent • primary • outcome • rare • concern • distress • limb
Farming words	meadow • nectar • nursery • orchard • blossom • plentiful • irrigation • cultivate •

Answer Key for Vocabulary Activity Pages

PLAY #1 ACTIVITY PAGES

Friendship words

WORD JUMBLE, *page 12*

1. lonely 2. courteous 3. loyal
4. dispute 5. cooperative 6. kind
7. share 8. considerate

CROSSWORD, *page 13*

Across 2. loyal 3. cooperative
5. dispute 7. considerate

Down 1. kind 2. lonely
4. courteous 6. share

PLAY #2 ACTIVITY PAGES

Neighborhood words

WORD JUMBLE, *page 18*

1. traffic 2. volunteer 3. statue
4. community 5. neighbor
6. pedestrian 7. mayor 8. stroll

CROSSWORD, *page 19*

Across 2. statue 3. volunteer
6. community 8. neighbor

Down 1. pedestrian 4. traffic
5. stroll 7. mayor

PLAY #3 ACTIVITY PAGES

Family words

WORD JUMBLE, *page 24*

1. tradition 2. cousin 3. grandfather
4. reunion 5. relative 6. aunt
7. festive 8. toddler

CROSSWORD, *page 25*

Across 1. grandfather 5. festive
6. aunt 7. reunion 8. toddler

Down 2. tradition 3. cousin
4. relative

PLAY #4 ACTIVITY PAGES

Big words, small words

WORD JUMBLE, *page 30*

1. length 2. height 3. humongous
4. minuscule 5. massive 6. colossal
7. miniature 8. gigantic

CROSSWORD, *page 31*

Across 1. height 3. massive
5. colossal 7. minuscule

Down 2. gigantic 3. minuscule
4. humongous 6. length

PLAY #5 ACTIVITY PAGES

Feeling words

WORD JUMBLE, *page 36*

1. confidence 2. grumpy 3.
embarrassed 4. miserable 5. proud
6. jealous 7. cozy 8. emotion

CROSSWORD, *page 37*

Across 3. emotion 5. miserable
6. jealous 7. confidence

Down 1. proud 2. cozy
3. embarrassed 4. grumpy

SYNONYM MATCH, *page 38*

1. cozy 2. miserable 3. proud
4. jealous 5. embarrassed
6. confidence 7. grumpy
8. emotion

FIND THE ANTONYM, *page 38*

1. self-doubt 2. cheerful
3. lack of feeling 4. uncomfortable
5. ashamed 6. delighted
7. thrilled 8. pleased

PLAY #6 ACTIVITY PAGES

Words for heroes and villains

WORD JUMBLE, *page 43*

1. vile 2. rescue 3. villain 4. coward
5. courageous 6. bravery
7. honor 8. evil

CROSSWORD, *page 44*

Across 6. villain 7. rescue

Down 1. courageous 2. bravery
3. coward 4. vile 5. honor 8. evil

SYNONYM MATCH, *page 45*

1. rescue 2. evil 3. honor 4. vile
5. bravery 6. coward 7. villain
8. courageous

FIND THE ANTONYM, *page 45*

1. desert 2. fearfulness 3. hero
4. good guy 5. delicious 6. disgrace
7. fearful 8. good

Movement words

WORD JUMBLE, *page 50*

1. spring 2. swiftly 3. sluggish
4. halt 5. dart 6. skid 7. soar
8. rapid

CROSSWORD, *page 51*

Across 2. soar 3. sluggish 5. rapid
6. dart

Down 1. spring 2. swift 3. skid
4. halt

Animal words

WORD JUMBLE, *page 62*

1. keen 2. pounce 3. nocturnal
4. enormous 5. venomous
6. scurry 7. species 8. predator

CROSSWORD, *page 63*

Across 1. pounce 3. species
5. venomous

Down 1. predator 2. keen
3. scurry 4. nocturnal 6. enormous

Weather words

WORD JUMBLE, *page 56*

1. blizzard 2. gust 3. forecast
4. sweltering 5. drizzle
6. temperature 7. humid
8. tornado

CROSSWORD, *page 57*

Across 3. gust 6. blizzard
7. temperature 8. tornado

Down 1. humid 2. drizzle
4. sweltering 5. forecast

Cooking words

WORD JUMBLE, *page 68*

1. dash 2. bon appetit 3. recipe
4. edible 5. apron 6. grind 7. boil
8. ingredient

CROSSWORD, *page 69*

Across 1. edible 6. apron 7. recipe
8. boil

Down 2. dash 3. bon appetit
4. grind 5. ingredient